# Firefighters

by Alison Behnke

Lerner Publications Company • Minneapolis

Lerner Publications Company
A division of Lerner Publishing Group
241 First Avenue North
Minneapolis, MN 55401 USA

Website address: www.lernerbooks.com

Words in **bold type** are explained in a glossary on page 31.

Library of Congress Cataloging-in-Publication Data

Behnke, Alison.
Firefighters / by Alison Behnke.
p. cm. – (Pull ahead books)
Includes index.
Summary: An introduction to the duties and daily life of fire fighters.
ISBN: 0–8225–0063–9 (lib. bdg. : alk. paper)
1. Fire extinction–Juvenile literature. [1. Fire fighters. 2. Occupations.] I. Title. II. Series.
TH9148.B45 2005
628.9'25–dc21 2003011203

Manufactured in the United States of America
1 2 3 4 5 6 – JR – 10 09 08 07 06 05

Do you see smoke?

Where is it coming from?

The smoke is from a burning building. Fire, fire!

Call the
firefighters!
They will help!

Firefighters put out fires. Fighting fires is dangerous work. Fires burn buildings and forests. They can also burn people.

Firefighters keep the **community** safe. Your community is made up of people in your neighborhood, town, or city.

Have you seen firefighters in your community? Some of them live at the fire station.

The station has beds to sleep in. It also has a kitchen. The firefighters cook their meals there.

Some fire stations have a pole from the second floor to the first floor.

What do you think the pole is for?

It lets firefighters move fast. They hear the call for help and slide down the pole. Then they quickly put on their **turnout gear.**

Turnout gear protects firefighters. A special suit keeps out heat. Other gear keeps smoke away.

Firefighters also wear **air tanks.**

In smoky buildings, they can breathe fresh air from these tanks.

Firefighters carry tools to fight fires. Cameras and goggles help them see through smoke. Axes help break through walls or windows.

A firefighter's outfit and tools weigh almost 30 pounds. That's as much as four or five backpacks full of books!

Time to go! The firefighters climb into the fire truck. It has hoses to spray water at fires. Some fire trucks have ladders to reach high places.

The fire truck's loud **siren** wails. Its lights flash. Cars get out of the way. The fire truck needs to get through!

The firefighters are here! They jump out of the truck and grab the hoses.

Firefighters shoot water at the flames.
Firefighters also **rescue** people.
They get them out of danger.

Firefighters help people during floods, bad storms, and other times of trouble.

Sometimes they help people who have been in car accidents too.

Firefighters teach people how to stay safe.

Firefighters show kids how to stop fires from starting. They also teach people how to get out of burning buildings safely.

Would you like to be a firefighter?
People take tests to become firefighters.

New firefighters go through **training.** Training teaches them how to fight fires safely.

Fighting fires is a big job. It is an important job.

Someday, maybe you will be a firefighter!

# Facts about Firefighters

- Men and women can be firefighters. The first female firefighter in the United States was hired in 1974.
- Firefighters need to exercise and stay fit. Firefighting is hard work!
- Every fire station has a **captain.** The captain leads the other firefighters and keeps the fire station running smoothly.
- Firefighters called **engineers** have special training. They help keep the fire truck running. They also drive the truck.
- Firefighters called **paramedics** have medical training. They can help people who are hurt or sick.

# Firefighters through History

Firefighting has always been important. But the ways that people fight fires have changed over the years.

- In the 1600s, people hung buckets by their front doors. When someone yelled “fire!” everyone filled their buckets with water. They passed the buckets down a line of people and poured the water on the fire. This was called a “bucket brigade.”

- Fire hydrants were invented in 1801. Firefighters could hook their hoses up to fire hydrants. Then they had plenty of water to squirt at a fire.

- The shiny red or yellow fire trucks that you have probably seen were not always around. Before cars were invented, firefighters rushed to emergencies in carriages pulled by horses.

# More about Firefighters

Check out these books and websites to find out more about firefighters. Or see if you can visit your local fire station. Maybe you will get to meet some real firefighters!

## Books

Hayward, Linda. *A Day in the Life of a Firefighter.* New York: Dorling Kindersley Publishing, 2001.

Jango-Cohen, Judith. *Fire Trucks.* Minneapolis, MN: Lerner Publications Company, 2003.

Jeunesse, Gallimard, and Daniel Moignot. *Fire Fighting.* New York: Scholastic, 1999.

Kottke, Jan. *A Day with Firefighters.* New York: Children's Press, 2000.

## Websites

*Fire Administration Kids Page*
<http://www.usfa.fema.gov/kids>

*Sparky the Fire Dog*
<http://www.nfpa.org/sparky>

# Glossary

**air tanks:** containers of clean air

**captain:** a firefighter who runs a fire station

**community:** a group of people who live in the same city, town, or neighborhood. Communities share the same fire departments, schools, libraries, and other helpful places.

**engineers:** firefighters who fix and drive fire trucks

**paramedics:** people who care for injured or sick people before they go to the hospital

**rescue:** to help a person get out of danger

**siren:** a loud horn on a fire truck

**training:** classes or practice to teach people how to do certain things

**turnout gear:** the clothes and tools that firefighters wear for protection

# Index



**Photo Acknowledgments**

The photographs in this book appear courtesy of: © Todd Strand/Independent Picture Service, front cover, pp. 10, 11, 16, 19; © Richard L. Carlton/Visuals Unlimited, pp. 3, 4; © Howard Ande, p. 5; © Todd Powell/Photo Network, p. 6; © Richard Renaldi/Visuals Unlimited, p. 7; © Warren Stone/Visuals Unlimited, p. 8; © Michael Heller/ 911 Pictures, pp. 9, 22; © Mark E. Gibson/Visuals Unlimited, pp. 12, 27; © Phyllis Picardi/Photo Network, p. 13; © Paul Halliday/911 Pictures, p. 14; © Kevin and Betty Collins/Visuals Unlimited, p. 15; © Patti McConville/Photo Network, p. 17; © Walton Smith/Photo Network, p. 18; © Doug Mazell/911 Pictures, p. 20; © Larry Stepanowicz/Visuals Unlimited, p. 21; © Timothy Tonge/911 Pictures, p. 23; © Bachmann/Photo Network, p. 24; © L. O'Shaughnessy/Visuals Unlimited, p. 25; © Jeff Greenberg/Visuals Unlimited, p. 26; © Visuals Unlimited, p. 29.